INTRODUCTION

We often take many of the human-made objects that surround us for granted. It is easy to forget that they are products of our ability to make use of the world's natural materials. Over the centuries, people have learned to adapt nature's raw materials and build from them the great variety of objects that make up our material wealth. Each object we manufacture is made from a part of the Earth's stock of natural materials, commonly referred to as resources. It is not only mineral supplies that qualify for the term resource. People need food and water, and the land, springs, plants and animals on which we depend have always been looked upon as important resources.

In advanced industrial societies like Britain, far more resources are used than anyone could have imagined even one hundred years ago. Furthermore, the number of people alive today is far greater than at any time in the world's history – and more people use more resources. Many experts predict that some of the most important resources will soon run out if we continue to use them at the present rate.

It now seems clear that our world faces a serious and immediate threat from the side effects of excessive resource exploitation. As we plough up more land, cut down more forests, burn more fuel and mine more minerals, not only are valuable resources depleted, but the environment is often polluted by the process of extraction. As the waste products from mines and factories pollute waterways, and as gases from car exhausts, power stations and factories pour into the air, we undermine the world's most important resources. Until recently, the world's atmosphere, oceans and ecosystems were taken for granted, but increasingly scientists are realising that clean air and water are the most vital resources of all, the resources that underpin life itself.

Chapter One

LIVING OFF THE FRUITS OF THE EARTH

The world is full of resources. Minerals, plants, animals and water have always been valuable resources for humans. When people first settled and began to farm, good, fertile soil became an important resource. Every time food passes our lips we are consuming some small part of the world's food resources. Each drink we take is drawn from the world's freshwater resources. Every part of a house and every object in it has been constructed using materials taken from nature and represents a minute portion of the world's material resources. Each time we turn on a light or start the car, we consume a small part of the energy resources available to us.

Thousands of years ago, humans exploited far fewer of the Earth's materials than we do today with our sophisticated technology. As more complex societies developed, the number of materials people could use grew, and an increasing number of the Earth's materials began to be seen in terms of the benefits they could yield.

Before people discovered how to mould clay into bricks to provide shelter and pots for storing food and water, clay probably seemed unimportant. Yet as soon as people learned how to turn this sticky substance into useful objects, it became a resource. Only 3,000 years ago, people discovered that they could make iron from a reddish rock. Following this discovery, iron rapidly became an enormously valuable metal and the source of power.

Where vital resources were less plentiful, people developed methods of controlling them to ensure their survival. In dry areas of the world, for example, people built complicated water storage and irrigation systems to make the most of a scarce resource. Today, the ways in which we manipulate the Earth's materials are far more sophisticated. It is difficult to imagine that all the materials used to make a television set have always been available. It

◁ Since people first settled and began to farm, technological innovation and the population explosion have led to a huge increase in the area of land under cultivation and to more intensive farming methods.

is only recently that we have developed the technology to turn those natural materials into a television. There is now very little for which people have not found a use. Industrialised society has become used to consuming products.

An insatiable demand for resources

Our demand on the Earth's resources is growing at a tremendous rate, and before long, we may exhaust the planet's supply of materials. In the developed world (Europe, Japan, North America and so on) people have more material possessions than ever, and are fast consuming the stocks of fossil fuels, minerals and other valuable materials. With so many people consuming such huge amounts, large-scale processes are required to extract enough energy, food, water and materials from the environment in order to satisfy demand.

Vast areas of land are dedicated to growing crops to feed city populations. Millions of litres of fresh water are drawn from rivers and lakes and pumped long distances to nourish crops and to keep people's toilets, washing machines, gardens and baths functioning. Mines burrow deep into the ground in search of coal that will be burned to provide electricity to light houses and streets and supply energy for the appliances we use. Oil platforms pump oil from the rocks under the sea. This oil then provides the energy that fuels an enormous fleet of cars. Oil also provides the raw material for the manufacture of plastics as well as many chemicals and medicines.

Quarries eat away whole mountain-sides to provide stone to build houses and roads, and huge lorries crawl out of pits laden with the metal ores needed to satisfy growing consumption. Chainsaws work night and day to fell the trees that provide us with wood and paper. Fleets of fishing boats haul millions of fish from the oceans. Our thirst for resources affects virtually every aspect of the world.

Side effects

Most of these activities cause damaging side effects. Intensive agriculture poisons our water supplies with fertilizers and pesticides. The new dams we build flood land that local people depend on for food, for instance in the Nile Valley. Mines leave behind huge mounds of waste that scar the landscape. The power stations and factories that process metal ores or crude oil release fumes into the atmosphere and waste into the rivers and seas. The more we consume, the faster we exploit resources and the faster we damage the environment. Even if we try to minimise the damage through controls, we cannot avoid it altogether.

Wealth and prosperity

Usually no visible resource shortage exists in the richer nations, but in many other countries there are serious shortages of even the most basic and vital resources. For instance, in the Sahel region of Africa firewood is very scarce and there are so many people searching for it that it can take a family a whole day to collect enough fuel for cooking. In the dry season, the same people often have to travel long distances in search of fresh water. In many countries, if a farmer cannot grow enough food for the family, they will go hungry and may even starve – a huge percentage of the world's population is undernourished.

Many people living in wealthy nations take it for granted that there will be food on the table, water gushing from the tap and fuel at an affordable price. Also, televisions, videos, radios and stereos have become common household goods. Yet it is clearly unjust that many people in developing countries do not have access to even the most meagre share of the world's resources.

Unequal distribution

There are many reasons why such imbalances exist in the distribution of resources around the world. Over the last three centuries, European and North American countries took over vast areas of the globe, tapping the natural resources they could find to build up their own industries. Although most of the former colonies are now independent, the world economic system still benefits those with the greatest financial wealth. As a result, the wealthiest nations buy a disproportionate amount of the world's raw materials.

It is very difficult for the poorer countries to compete economically, and they get left behind as the consumer societies of the richer nations absorb more and more of the available resources. However, this is not the only reason why the rich countries are getting richer and the poor ones poorer. In many developing countries, internal instability, for instance civil wars and government inefficiency and corruption, damages their economic prospects.

△ In some areas of the world, people do not even have the resources to feed themselves. Above, food is distributed in Ethiopia.

▷ Meanwhile, in New York City, shops are packed with luxury goods.

△ The more people compete for goods, the more strain is placed on resources.

The population explosion

The world population explosion is another factor which prevents people in the poorer nations from getting a larger share of the available resources. It is clear that if more people compete for limited resources, the less there will be to go round. As a result, increasing strain is placed on the systems that provide those resources. For instance, as a growing number of people search for firewood, the forests that provide it are gradually destroyed. As trees are removed, the soil is loosened by erosion from wind and rain. In the worst cases, previously fertile land may be turned into desert.

On the surface it looks as though wealthy, consumer-oriented societies degrade the environment in a different way than the impoverished African farmer. In fact the root causes of environmental degradation are very similar. In both cases, the delicate balance between population, environment and resources is stretched to the limit. Maintaining this balance is crucial to the success of people around the world.

Energy (mostly in the form of sunlight) and a few meteorites are the only resources that the Earth receives from the rest of the universe. This means that, excluding energy, the world is a closed system. The human race has sent astronauts to the moon and spacecraft to probe distant planets, but we do not yet have the technology to exploit the minerals on other planets and it would be irresponsible to attempt it. For this reason, the resources available to us are limited to what we have on Earth.

Renewable or non-renewable?

The world's resources fall into two basic categories; those that are renewable and those that are non-renewable. The availability of both types is limited, but in very different ways. Once non-renewable materials are extracted from the environment, the resource is gone permanently. Renewable materials, on the other hand, can be continually generated and the main factor limiting their availability is the rate at which they can be produced.

There are many examples of both renewable and non-renewable resources. The crude oil drawn from the ground which is vital as a source of energy is a non-renewable resource. The processes that create oil take millions of years. Once oil is pumped out of the Earth and burned, it is gone forever. The implications of this are that when the most easily accessible oil resources are used up, we will have to look for sources that are harder and more expensive to tap. Eventually, oil could become very scarce indeed. Firewood, on the other hand, is a renewable resource, as a healthy forest will continue producing new trees every year. In a well-balanced situation, the sustainable resource is the amount of firewood that can be gathered without damaging the forest. If the forest is too damaged, the trees (and the firewood) disappear.

There is currently a lot of interest in developing the potential of renewable resources; if properly managed they can last indefinitely. Renewable energy supplies are particularly important, as they are less damaging environmentally than the fossil fuels that we currently depend on.

△ Power – but not for all in South Africa

Limits to growth

In the 1960s, some scientists began to point out that the world economy could not continue to grow explosively because of limited resources. As consumption grows, fuelled by population growth and higher incomes, so the rate at which we use up the world's resources accelerates. Scientists produced reports showing how fast some resources were being depleted. They also predicted that some vital non-renewable resources would soon run out because people were consuming so much.

Economic growth relies on availability of resources, which is hard to calculate. Estimates of how much of a particular resource is left are based on the amount which can be profitably extracted from the environment. But this quantity changes all the time. As a resource becomes rarer and harder to extract, prices will rise and previously unprofitable supplies will be

tapped, expanding the amount of that resource. For example, if the price of gold were to rise, it might become economically feasible to extract the minute traces of gold commonly found in sea-water.

Another reason why it is very difficult to predict how long a resource will last is that we do not know how materials will be used in the future. If we can learn to use less of each material, and if we can substitute common materials for rare ones, or renewable materials for non-renewable ones, resources will last much longer. If, where possible, non-renewable resources are recycled instead of thrown away, this will also protect supplies.

A here and now approach

Currently, economic planners are short-sighted. If a resource is considered profitable it will be exploited now, even though this may mean that the accessible supplies will soon run out. This is how so many precious resources are squandered – just look at the materials we commonly throw away: glass, tin cans, newspapers and

△ Two thousand million people rely on wood for their fuel.

so on. Many of them could easily be recycled, but since they are made from materials which are currently relatively cheap to extract from the environment, it is just as easy for us to discard them and replace them with new supplies. The lack of foresight with which we use up valuable resources is like someone embarking on a long desert crossing and drinking all his or her water on the first day.

Many people are becoming more aware that the world's limited resources are being wasted and they are calling for people worldwide to develop sustainably. A sustainable society is one which uses its resources in such a way that it can maintain its standard of living into the future. This not only means conserving and recycling non-renewable resources; it also means making sure that human activities do not destroy the environment on which renewable resources depend.

A lesson from yeast
When yeast is introduced into a bucket of warm, sugary water, it rapidly multiplies.

As the yeast feeds on the sugar, it produces two waste products; carbon dioxide and alcohol. The carbon dioxide escapes into the atmosphere, while most of the alcohol stays in the bucket. There are two possible results. First, as the yeast multiplies, it consumes food at an ever-increasing rate. Eventually, when all the sugar is used up, the yeast dies of starvation. In the second scenario, there is no shortage of sugar. The hungry yeast continues to feed, multiply and produce waste products. Eventually, the yeast comes to a grisly end, drowned in its own waste.

The predicament of the human race is in many ways rather similar to that of the yeast in warm water. We may be able to expand our population and our consumption until we run short of vital resources. On the other hand, we may find that the pollution we produce as we use up the world's resources will destroy our environment – and us – before then. But there is another option open to us. The yeast does not have the intelligence to control its population explosion and its consumption; we do.

Resources: use and abuse

Almost everywhere we have searched, humans have discovered resources from which we have created the objects that surround us. A bird's eye view reveals the extent of resource exploitation by humans. Tightly-packed towns and villages, huge factories belching smoke, vast patchworks of emerald, yellow or bare fields and ragged forests are all, in one way or another, the product or side effect of exploitation of the Earth's limited resources.

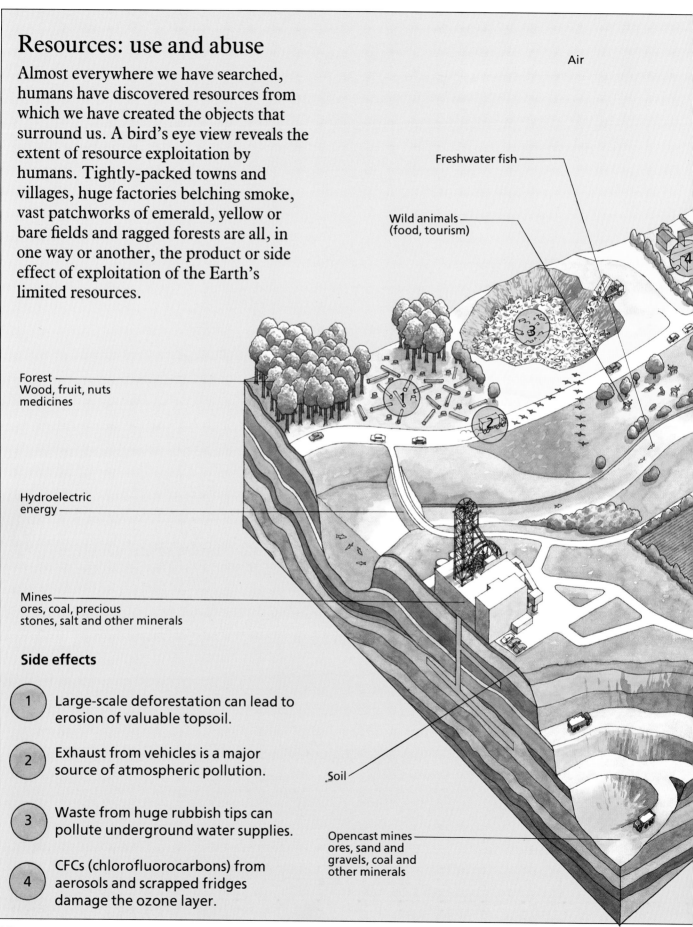

Air

Freshwater fish

Wild animals
(food, tourism)

Forest
Wood, fruit, nuts
medicines

Hydroelectric
energy

Mines
ores, coal, precious
stones, salt and other minerals

Soil

Opencast mines
ores, sand and
gravels, coal and
other minerals

Side effects

1   Large-scale deforestation can lead to erosion of valuable topsoil.

2   Exhaust from vehicles is a major source of atmospheric pollution.

3   Waste from huge rubbish tips can pollute underground water supplies.

4   CFCs (chlorofluorocarbons) from aerosols and scrapped fridges damage the ozone layer.

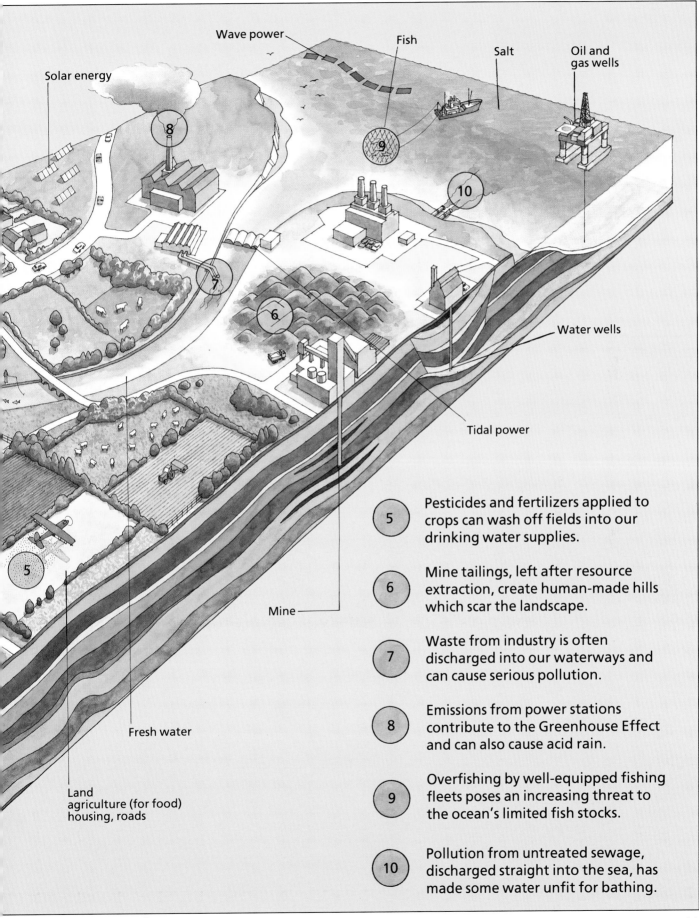

Wave power

Fish

Salt

Oil and gas wells

Solar energy

Water wells

Tidal power

Mine

Fresh water

Land agriculture (for food) housing, roads

5 Pesticides and fertilizers applied to crops can wash off fields into our drinking water supplies.

6 Mine tailings, left after resource extraction, create human-made hills which scar the landscape.

7 Waste from industry is often discharged into our waterways and can cause serious pollution.

8 Emissions from power stations contribute to the Greenhouse Effect and can also cause acid rain.

9 Overfishing by well-equipped fishing fleets poses an increasing threat to the ocean's limited fish stocks.

10 Pollution from untreated sewage, discharged straight into the sea, has made some water unfit for bathing.

Chapter Two

RESOURCES HERE, THERE AND EVERYWHERE

We have developed uses for a vast number of natural materials. Advances in technology have meant that more of the world's materials can be processed into objects. Every part of the land, ocean and air contains something that, potentially at least, we can use. Many resources are exploited to provide comforts which people in developed nations have become accustomed to. However, these luxuries could cost us dear in the long run if they threaten other resources which provide the basic necessities vital to human survival. Many people believe that things are going wrong, and this is why the "green movement" has been growing in importance.

Minerals

When people think about resources, the first things that usually come to mind are minerals. Minerals, which are non-renewable, are the basic building blocks for many of the material possessions we surround ourselves with. The discovery by Stone Age people thousands of years ago that flints could be fashioned into useful tools was a revolutionary step. Later on, the mastering of fire led to the discovery that certain rocks could yield metals. Humans benefitted greatly from using metals to make tools and weapons to exploit the environment. Mineral resources, together with the technology to process them, gave people great power as they still do today.

Gradually, more metals were discovered, but the methods of extracting and processing them from the ores remained difficult. However, after the Industrial Revolution in the 18th century, more complex methods of surveying for ore deposits and machinery to help in mines and foundries were developed. Metals became cheaper and began to be used widely throughout society.

Metals are by no means the only minerals we use. People have been hewing stones in order to build homes and monuments for thousands of years. Later they learned to make bricks from clay. In Britain, bricks, mortar and cement were first introduced by the Romans, who started the exploitation of some of our mineral resources which continues to this day. Huge quantities of sand, gravel, limestone and rock are excavated and quarried every year. Economically, these building materials are the most important minerals in Britain.

Sodium chloride, or common salt, is another important mineral. A person generally uses about five kg every year and huge quantities of it are used in the chemical industry and to keep roads ice-free during cold weather.

△ Only 4,000 years ago tools were carved from stone.

▷ Today most are forged from metal ores.

Fossil fuels

There are other important resources buried in the Earth's crust. The fossil fuels (oil, gas and coal) are all extracted from the ground. Before the Industrial Revolution people used wood as fuel, but industry's increased consumption meant that trees simply could not grow fast enough to provide the quantities of fuel required. Coal mines were developed to tap the Earth's coal resources. Coal is fossilised wood. It is the remains of ancient swampy forests buried millions of years ago. Just as wood contains solar energy (energy from the Sun) trapped by trees over the last few decades, so coal represents solar energy trapped and buried for millions of years. Like metal ores, coal is either excavated from deep mines or from opencast mines (open to the air) at the Earth's surface.

Oil is also a form of fossilised solar energy. It is formed from the remains of microscopic organisms that died and sank to the murky ocean floors millions of years ago. It is less than a century since large-scale extraction of oil began. Now there are oil fields in many countries and demand seems insatiable. Every day the world's car fleet grows. Oil is not only valuable as fuel, but also forms the basis of the petrochemical industry which manufactures many plastics, as well as chemicals used in medicines, pesticides, detergents and so on.

Most of the wealth in modern industrial society is derived from materials excavated from the Earth's crust. Ten thousand years ago, when the first flint mines were developed, the world's five million or so inhabitants made only minimal demands on underground resources. Now there are over five thousand million people on Earth, and many are surrounded by a variety of possessions that have been moulded from

◁ Opencast mining of brown coal destroys the landscape. Burning brown coal contributes to global warming and produces acid rain.

▽ Cups and saucers are produced from china clay. This heap has been left behind after clay extraction in Cornwall.

the huge array of materials we have learned to draw from the Earth. The scale of the processes of extraction is enormous and the side effects threaten to be very serious.

Scarring the landscape

The scale of extraction creates a number of serious environmental problems. When opencast mines and quarries are developed, they leave huge and ugly scars on the landscape and heaps of waste that can tower hundreds of metres. Until recently, when mines and quarries were exhausted, great holes were simply left behind. Today, more effort is made to landscape them afterwards and, where possible, return them to a visibly acceptable state. Although such aesthetic considerations are gaining ground

in some of the wealthy nations, in most developing countries they remain low on the list of priorities.

In Britain, some 2,000 hectares of land are destroyed by mineral extraction every year – the size of a medium town. There is already a huge amount of unusable land in Britain as a result of two centuries of mineral resource exploitation. There is an increasing conflict between the image of a green and pleasant land and the need for more materials to build houses, schools, hospitals and roads, and to supply the ores and energy needed to satisfy industry. In addition, land lost by excavation and building means less land for growing food. Competition for land between developers and farmers is a growing problem.

The Greenhouse Effect

Vast amounts of energy are needed to convert resources into useful objects. This energy is likely to come from burning fossil fuels. As more resources are exploited, the amount of fossil fuels burned increases and more pollutants pour into the atmosphere. There is increasing unease about the rate at which we burn fossil fuels and the possible damaging effects of gases rising into the atmosphere.

As a result of burning large amounts of fossil fuels, the level of carbon dioxide in the atmosphere is rising rapidly and many scientists believe that this will lead to global warming, commonly known as the Greenhouse Effect. As yet the consequences of such warming are unclear, but they could include changes in climate around the world, involving more droughts, floods and hurricanes, as well as rising sea levels which could flood many heavily populated and fertile coastal areas.

It is difficult to reduce the amount of carbon dioxide released when fossil fuels are burned. The only realistic way of reducing the amount of carbon dioxide emitted into our atmosphere is simply to burn less coal, oil and gas.

△ It is estimated that the damage to crops and forests caused by acid rain costs Europe more than $10 billion a year. The Black Forest in Germany is badly damaged.

Acid rain

Scientists estimate that some 100 million tonnes of sulphur dioxide and nitric oxide are poured into the atmosphere every year from exhaust pipes and chimneys. When these gases react with rainwater they produce acid rain which damages trees, crops, buildings and human and animal health. To halve the emission of these gases before the end of the century would cost EEC countries at least $5 billion every year until then.

World economic inequality

In the developed world, strict measures are being introduced to control pollution. Yet in many developing countries, the cost of pollution prevention measures means that usually little is done, and people and the environment suffer the consequences.

The problems are greatest in the poorest nations. Many have not yet developed the industry or transport networks to process their natural resources – many simply do not have the money to do so. The economies of many of the poorer nations depend on the export of their ores and minerals to the richer, industrialised nations. The industrial countries use these raw materials to produce expensive end-products which the poorer countries then spend their hard-earned foreign currency buying back.

Matters are made even more difficult for the poorer nations by fierce worldwide competition and prices going up and down on the mineral markets. For a country dependent on the price of its ore, a drop in its value can be devastating. It is not surprising, then, that so many countries are reluctant to spend money to protect the environment. If they were to invest in technologies that reduce pollution and environmental degradation, the resources they sell would earn them even less profit and only leave them poorer.

Other damaging effects

New technologies are constantly being developed and this, together with an insatiable demand for minerals, means that new and often lower-grade ore deposits are continually being exploited. When lower-grade resources are developed, more ore has to be extracted in order to produce every tonne of metal. This means that more energy is needed to process the ore and the environmental impact of resource exploitation is increased.

The minerals and fossil fuels we extract from the ground form the basis of modern industrial society. Although they are the source of much pollution and environmental degradation, there are many other types of resource use that also seriously damage the environment.

Freshwater pollution

Water is a vital resource – without water, there would be no life on Earth. In wet countries, such as those in Northern Europe, people assume that clean water will flow from the tap and that there will always be enough to drink, clean the house and water the garden. Only during the occasional long, dry summer do supplies run short, and even then, there is always enough to allow us to eat and drink.

However, the provision of such huge amounts of clean water in a land as densely populated as ours is far from simple. Every drop of water we use first fell as rain. As rain washes over fields, flows along city gutters and makes its way towards streams, rivers, lakes and reservoirs, it can pick up dangerous chemicals and germs. Water pollution is a serious problem.

Water pollution is generally the result of the methods employed in exploiting other resources. The effluent from factories processing minerals and chemicals, the fertilizers and pesticides washed from the fields and the poisons washed from

enormous rubbish tips are all caused by other forms of resource use. While growing industry and agriculture often pollute fresh water, they also demand increasing amounts of clean water, thus it becomes harder to protect water supplies. This is why strict water pollution-control measures are now being introduced.

Polluting the seas

The seas and oceans contain valuable resources. The livelihood of fishermen around the world depends on the health of fish stocks. There are real fears that pollution may be undermining this marine resource. For centuries, we have simply drained and dumped our unwanted wastes into the huge seas and oceans, assuming that they would disappear without seriously damaging the environment. However, industries around the world expand, and more and more waste has to be disposed of, so the oceans and seas are suffering. In the shallow, enclosed seas like the North Sea, many scientists believe that pollution may already have reached a critical stage and may lie at the root of recent fish and sea mammal disease epidemics.

Overfishing

Overfishing in many areas of the world is leading to reduced populations of fish. New fishing methods, like the introduction of motorised fleets in the developing world, might boost catches in the short term, but in the long run, hauls may drop rapidly for fishermen worldwide.

In the Pacific, for example, drift nets are causing massive destruction of sea life. Every night hundreds of huge nets are dropped, each one up to 50 km long. These nets are intended to catch tuna and squid, but in practice they kill anything that swims into them – they have been nicknamed Walls of Death. Although they have been introduced only in the last few years, there are already fears that they could lead to the extinction of many species. Fish are a renewable resource, but they are most useful when exploited at a sustainable rate. If we catch all the fish in the oceans today, there will be none left for tomorrow.

◁ △ While people have developed complex schemes for controlling water for their use, they often fail to protect water and the plants and animals that live in it against the ravages of pollution such as effluents from industries and oil spills.

△ Lake Chad's receding shoreline shows how serious recent droughts have been.

△ Those who can afford it develop complex systems to get around water shortages.

Water shortage

Many countries face water resource problems that are very different from ours. Their problems are associated not so much with water quality, but with quantity. They need water for a growing population, as well as for expanding agriculture and industry. Many countries, for example the Sudan, receive very little rainfall, and finding enough fresh water is a real problem. The media shows us the effects of drought – millions fleeing their land in search of food. This is a tragic case of a resource not able to keep up with the need of the people.

In a wealthy nation like the United States, farmers try to find technological shortcuts around water shortages by developing huge and expensive irrigation schemes. But this too can bring problems. Their source of water is often groundwater from wells, and this is essentially a finite resource. Although much groundwater is renewable, the amount used must not

exceed the rate at which rainwater fills the underground reservoirs. In many places, so much water is being pumped out of the ground that water reserves are being depleted fast.

In other cases, groundwater was sealed into the rocks thousands of years ago. Many dry areas are dependent on this fossil water for their survival, but the resource cannot last indefinitely.

Clearing the forests

Forests are rich in resources. The most obvious one is wood, which provides valuable fuel and material for building, furnishing and paper making. People have exploited trees through the ages. Only a few centuries ago, much of Britain was forested; now only four per cent of the land is wooded. Forests were cleared to make way for farming and wood was used for construction and fuel before the discovery of fossil fuels. Britain is by no means the

18

only country in the world to have lost large parts of its forest resources. Much of Europe has been deforested, and as Europeans gained influence in other continents, large areas of North America, Australia, New Zealand and South Africa were also cleared.

Deforestation is continuing. Demand for valuable hardwoods (and plain old chipboard) contributes to the felling of huge areas of tropical rainforest in Asia, Africa and South and Central America. However, this is not the only pressure leading to the clearing of the forests. Growing populations need more land, and in many areas forests are felled to make way for agriculture or to search for underground mineral resources. There is growing concern about this. The soils in which many tropical forests grow are often poor. When land is deforested, soils are left vulnerable to erosion, and heavy rain can strip off valuable topsoil in just a few years, causing floods and creating human-made wastelands. Concern is mounting that if the forests are destroyed, what is left behind may be of little use to anyone.

Sustainable forest use
Presently, hundreds of trees are destroyed to gain access to just a handful of valuable trees. Careful logging of only the biggest and best trees would allow forests to go on producing useful woods indefinitely.

Other forest resources also exist. Many tropical forest trees bear potentially valuable fruit and nut crops. Some produce latex, the basis for the rubber industry. The forests are very rich in different plant and animal species, some of which have not even been catalogued. These may provide the basic ingredients for new foods, drinks, medicines and pesticides. Every species made extinct is a resource lost forever.

Scientists are also concerned that deforestation may be contributing significantly to the Greenhouse Effect.

△ Parts of Nepal were once densely forested.

Extinction
Although tropical rainforests cover only six per cent of the Earth's land surface, they could contain as many as 90 per cent of the world's plant and animal species. Already almost half of the original rainforests have been destroyed, and thousands of species made extinct.

Trees grow by using sunlight to absorb carbon dioxide from the atmosphere, and then releasing oxygen. As trees are cut down and burned, huge amounts of carbon dioxide are released into the atmosphere. As carbon dioxide is the main greenhouse gas, the concern is that deforestation may contribute to global warming.

Soil
Some areas of grassland are natural; others have been created over the centuries by humans clearing the forests. These areas

△ Dust in the United States in the 1930s.

provide our main source of food. Animals graze on grasslands, and croplands are ploughed to grow cereals and vegetables. The main resource of these areas is the soil, which contains the nutrients plants need.

Topsoil is the nutrient-rich top layer of earth in which plants grow. Without it, we could not feed ourselves. Topsoil takes hundreds of years to form; on a human timescale it is a non-renewable resource. In many parts of the world, soil is being eroded at a frightening rate. This resource vital to our survival is being lost.

Erosion
Soil loss is frequently associated with deforestation. Forest vegetation holds the soil together and helps water drain into it. When trees are removed, rain falls directly onto the soil and runs along the surface taking earth with it. In some places, the rate at which soil is being lost is very rapid. For example, in the United States, billions of tonnes are being eroded from the fields every year. Huge gullies, sometimes tens of metres deep, can be carved out of fields in just a few years. When the topsoil is eroded, farmers have to rely much more on chemical fertilizers to grow crops. In areas

of the world where farmers only just manage to make a living, they cannot afford artificial aids. In these countries, soil erosion can lead to reduced crop yields, making people even poorer. In extreme cases, soil loss can lead to famine.

Soil is not only eroded by water. Probably the most famous case of soil erosion was the Dust Bowl of the 1930s in the midwestern United States. A series of hot, dry summers reduced soil, bared by overgrazing and ploughing, to dust. The winds threw up huge dust clouds, "black blizzards", stripping the land of soil. Erosion can be prevented by keeping plant or tree cover over the soil to protect it from heavy rains and wind.

Energy from the Sun
Sunlight, or solar energy, keeps the atmosphere warm and stimulates the chemical reactions that convert carbon dioxide and water into carbohydrates in plants – the basic food for all life forms. This process is known as photosynthesis. Solar energy is a resource upon which all life depends.

The Sun's energy drives wind, waves and running water. Technologies for extracting the energy from these renewable sources are becoming more sophisticated. Huge modern wind turbines already provide large amounts of electricity in some parts of the world. Prototype wave machines are being tested and hydroelectricity has already been exploited in many countries, particularly in France. Technologies also exist for extracting energy directly from sunlight, either as electricity from solar cells or as hot water for heating homes and greenhouses. Environmentalists hope that in the future solar energy resources can provide clean alternatives to fossil fuels.

Energy from the elements
Nuclear energy does not produce acid rain

△ Wind is a source of renewable energy.

△ Machines took jobs from many.

or contribute to the Greenhouse Effect, but the environmental dangers of nuclear waste and the threat of accidents make many people uneasy about using uranium (a radioactive element used in nuclear power) as the basis for energy supply.

Other potential energy resources are geothermal energy, which uses the heat in rocks deep in the Earth, and tidal energy which depends on tides in special areas like the Severn estuary.

Fresh air?

We live surrounded by air and take breaths of it about 20 times a minute, day and night, throughout our lives. Is it surprising that we take the atmosphere for granted and tend to forget that it is a resource without which we would die?

We have all seen dirty factories spewing out foul smoke and cars emitting choking fumes, as well as aerosol spray cans unleashing gases into the air. Until recently, we forgot how dependent we are on the atmosphere and believed it was something so huge that human activity could not inflict any serious damage.

But what about acid rain, which kills fish and plants in lakes and rivers, destroys huge areas of forest, and is harmful to people? What about the Greenhouse Effect and the fact that industrial and agricultural activities are releasing so many gases into the atmosphere that they are changing the composition of the air itself? Have we not seen the satellite maps of the ozone hole? This hole was created by chemicals invented less than a century ago, but released in sufficient quantities to undermine the barrier that protects us from the most harmful rays of the Sun.

Perceptions are changing fast. We are increasingly realising that the invisible atmosphere separating us from empty space is an essential resource – a part of nature we must look after because it is a resource we cannot live without.

Labour

People themselves are a resource. Ultimately, it is the work of people that moulds other resources to their needs. Often, the human resource (labour) is overlooked. Expensive and energy-intensive machinery is sometimes used to carry out work that could just as effectively be done by people. All too often, the result is high levels of unemployment.

Investing in new equipment is only sensible if it enables people to raise their standard of living by producing more out of their work. By making better use of the skills of the majority, many developing countries could improve the standard of living of their whole population rather than just a privileged few.

Chapter Three

LIFESTYLES

There are huge differences in the lifestyles of people around the world. The main reason for this is the distribution of wealth. The physical objects that make up our material wealth are all, in one way or another, made from natural materials drawn from the world's limited resources. In the richer nations, people surround themselves with appliances which are far removed from the natural materials used to make them, and which take a lot of energy to produce. In many areas of the world, people can only dream of the kind of wealth many people in North America and Europe enjoy. The peasant farmers or manual labourers in the poorer nations have very limited access to their share of the world's resources.

△ Many resources are used to build homes.

In Europe, almost all households have at least one television set and most have a colour one. In many areas of the world an old black and white TV in a village hall can still attract the population of an entire village. The idea of owning a TV is, for many, symbolic of great wealth – many people do not even have access to the electricity they would need to run one.

The best way to appreciate the extreme differences in the level of material wealth around the world is to examine all the objects that surround us. In the developing nations most of these objects are owned only by the very richest people.

Outside a house
Imagine you are standing outside a typical house in the area you live in. It is a type of house that could be in the country or in a town. Its owners, a family of four, might be farmers, but it is equally possible that they might work in a factory or a bank. The house is made of red brick (it could have been stone or concrete). The windows are made of wood and glass, they àre painted

△ Resources from around the world are used.

and are well-cleaned. The house has a red-tiled or slate roof. There is nothing peculiar about this home; it is the type of building we walk past every day.

But just think how many materials were used in its construction. There are thousands of bricks and hundreds of roof tiles, each one excavated from a clay pit, moulded into shape and baked in a huge furnace. Perhaps the bricks were made some distance away and have been transported here by lorries, using a lot of fuel in the process. Each brick is cemented into place – how many bags of cement did it take to build this house? The extraction of the clay and limestone used to build this house has left a hole somewhere. The front doors and windows are made of wood and so are the beams that hold up the roof. Inside, the floorboards are wooden; quite a few trees must have been felled to build this home. The glass was made from sand fused in a furnace. The paint is basically oil from deep underground, processed, put into tins and brought here to spread over the walls.

There are millions of houses like this.

Millions of tonnes of clay were moulded into millions of bricks and tiles, forests of trees sawn into hectares of floorboards, beams and doors. Millions of tonnes of sand were processed into enough glass to fit every window in the country, and millions of litres of paint were manufactured from the raw materials provided by nature.

Inside a home
Every floor is covered with a thick carpet. In this house the carpet is made from artificial fibre; another petrochemical product. The walls are covered with paper – the product of pulped trees. Most of the furniture is made of wood. Some of it is made from indigenous trees like pine, oak or ash, but most of it was originally carved from the heart of the rainforest and has been carried here across thousands of kilometres by road and ship. In the kitchen, most of the surfaces are covered with heat-resistant plastic, another petrochemical product. Cupboards contain iron, steel or copper pans moulded from ores mined in distant lands.

23

The house is lit by a multitude of light bulbs, each one delicately fashioned out of glass, tungsten and ceramics. Throughout the country there are millions of bulbs in offices and homes, all needing replacement every few months. Each one may not weigh very much, but the materials contained in a light bulb are not the only resources used to make them. Making glass and ceramics, forging tungsten and other metals and putting them all together to form a beautifully created but disposable object takes a huge amount of energy. As a general rule, the more distant an object is from the raw materials used to make it, the more energy is needed in its construction.

Many appliances in the house make the light bulb look distinctly simple. There is a colour television set, an oven, a fridge, washing machine, sewing machine, vacuum cleaner and a microwave – even a computer. These appliances have thousands of components, each one carefully crafted for a particular purpose. There are hundreds of different materials: metals, enamels, paints and plastics, all forged from the world's natural resources and all requiring massive amounts of energy for their mining, processing and assembly. There are so many objects in the house representing so many materials drawn from so many sources and moulded in so many ways that it would take a library of books to list all of them.

Outside the house, there is a car. It is difficult to appreciate that this machine was built almost entirely from metal ores and crude oil. This car will join millions of other fuel-guzzling machines on the road.

▷ *Above*: Every car is built from huge amounts of metal, rubber and plastic. It will burn thousands of litres of fuel and needs access to thousands of kilometres of roads.

▷ Food in this North American supermarket has been processed and packaged.

Resources on tap

The material possessions of a family are not the only resources they use. The house is also centrally heated. Gas, tapped from rocks hundreds of kilometres away, travels through a complex system of pipes into the house, to be burned for heat. Electricity, drawn from a network of wires criss-crossing the country, powers the electrical appliances. Every time the tap is turned and clear water runs out, a complex system of resource use is called upon. The water is pumped through a sophisticated system of purification and chlorination until, after travelling along many kilometres of pipe, it flows from the kitchen or bathroom tap.

Food

The larder, fridge and freezer are well-stocked. Some of the foods, like rice and vegetables, are scarcely different from the produce harvested on the farms where it grew. Most of the food, however, is heavily processed and packaged. There are stocks of tinned foods – small amounts of nutrition packed inside containers of valuable metal, mined, refined and moulded only to be thrown away once their contents have been consumed. There are biscuits wrapped in silver foil, paper and plastic; all resources that will only be used once.

Many families in Europe eat meat at least once a day. Most of the meat consumed is from livestock that has been intensively reared. In other words, the animals were fed on grains and other manufactured foods. It takes several kilograms of grain to make just one kilogram of meat, and the grain would have made nutritious food for humans in the first place.

All the food in the house is produced using intensive modern agricultural methods – this family does not eat "organic" food. Thousands of tonnes of fertilizers and pesticides were spread on the fields. The whole process was heavily mechanised using tractors and combine harvesters. The food industry uses huge factories to process metals and parts for machinery. An extremely complex and organised system has evolved that exploits resources from around the world, all building upon each other to bring us the foods we consume.

▷ Many people live in abject poverty and the situation is getting worse. In 1984, the average income in the poorer nations was only $190, compared to $11,430 in the industrialised countries. These shanty-town dwellings are in Hong Kong where living space is very crowded.

Home from another country

Not all people are as fortunate as the family described. The home of a peasant farmer in a developing country is likely to be much more simple. It is probably a low, one-storey building. The home has a rugged look about it and has been built from clay bricks, made locally and by hand. The two windows on either side of the wooden door are small – very little glass has been used to glaze them. The roof is made of handmade tiles; it could just as easily have been thatched. All the materials have been manufactured locally since there is little money with which to import materials. You could build ten or more of these houses out of the resources used in the construction of a single home in a wealthy country.

25

Inside, the floor is made of clay, spread smoothly and allowed to dry. There is very little furniture. In one room there is a clay oven fuelled by firewood. There is also a small kerosene stove and a lamp. As far as kitchen appliances go, there is little more than a few aluminium pots, a grinding stone, knives and two plastic buckets for water. There is no well-stocked larder, just a bag of rice and a few beans, vegetables and some oil. In the other room, where the whole family sleeps, there are three wooden beds, no mattresses, and a pile of neatly folded blankets. Except for a few items like a watch, a few simple tools, an old radio, the plastic buckets and some synthetic clothing, the house and all its contents were forged directly by hand.

Outside, there is no car waiting. Perhaps there is a bicycle; most likely the family walks, taking the bus on longer journeys. Water is drawn directly from a village well – there is no complex system of purification and distribution. Most of the food is cultivated nearby, although some of the grain was imported since not enough is grown locally. Few chemicals or machines were involved in growing and harvesting the food.

This house is not unlike many others in poor farming communities. A city home in a developing country would look decidedly different. For one thing, it would contain more manufactured goods and less local products. Nevertheless, the family would consume far fewer resources than people in the wealthier nations do.

Machines to make machines to make machines...

Comparing the lifestyles of wealthy and poor people illustrates different resource use. The resources used to build and decorate a house are only the tip of the iceberg. In industrial countries, the methods used to make machines to process

△ These water carriers in Chad spend several hours a day fetching water from the nearest well. In the developing world unsafe water kills some 60 million people a year.

raw materials are all very resource intensive. The whole system is a complex network, each part depending on another and all depending on a limitless supply of materials and energy resources. To feed this system, we import materials from around the world and transport them thousands of kilometres. Many resources end up as objects which are of very little practical value. It is now common to exploit resources from places that, two hundred years ago, we did not even know existed.

In comparison, a Third World family uses very few imported products. Most of its materials are local. The processes used to turn the resources into useful goods are simple, and therefore the rate of resource use is much lower.

A limit to material wealth

Since the world's resources are limited, it will never be possible for every family in the world to live in the type of European home we described. The intensity of resource use needed for that lifestyle would simply not be possible on a global scale. This is particularly true in view of the rate at which the world's population is increasing.

It is clear that many systems in both the wealthier and poorer nations are currently not sustainable. In Britain and other wealthy nations, the rate at which we consume resources means that we cannot keep going as we are – the strains placed on the environment are simply too great. Waste products created by resource exploitation are already beginning to poison our soils, water and atmosphere, possibly permanently. In the poorer nations, despite much lower resource use, problems are still huge. The strain placed on natural systems by an expanding population trying to eke out a living is destroying the resources that people depend on for their very survival.

It is time to rethink the relationship between people, material wealth and the environment. We must learn how to use the world's rich resources on an equitable, sustainable basis.

△ In developing countries many people rely on bicycles or buses for transport.

△ Salt miners use traditional mining techniques and their wages are very low.

Poverty

In 1980 there were more hungry people than at any other time in history. The proportion of people without access to adequate food, shelter and clothing has grown. Some 70 per cent of the people of sub-Saharan Africa do not get the calories they need to stay healthy. Every day, thousands of people in the world die because they have not received their share of the most basic resources.

Wasteful use

There is no sign that people are beginning to use resources more carefully – all the evidence suggests quite the opposite. As growing populations demand more resources, the strains we place on our environment increase. In coming decades, many of the basic resources we depend on may not be able to keep up with demand, and many renewable resources will have been depleted by overuse. It is vital that people develop sustainable lifestyles and societies now, before it is too late. We must all learn to make better use of resources and avoid creating a world in which soil, air and water are seriously degraded, and in which shortages of even the most basic resources are an everyday reality.

Our waterways

Excessive demand, in addition to pollution from industry, agriculture, sewage and domestic waste, is placing intolerable strains on our waterways and causing considerable damage. Yet wholesome water resources are essential to our very existence.

Water

The lifestyles of many in wealthy nations demand huge amounts of water compared to those in developing countries. Water resources worldwide are already under pressure from current demands. For many, there seems little prospect of ever having as much water as they need. There is a very real risk that countries desperate for water might start wars, in an attempt to get access to new supplies.

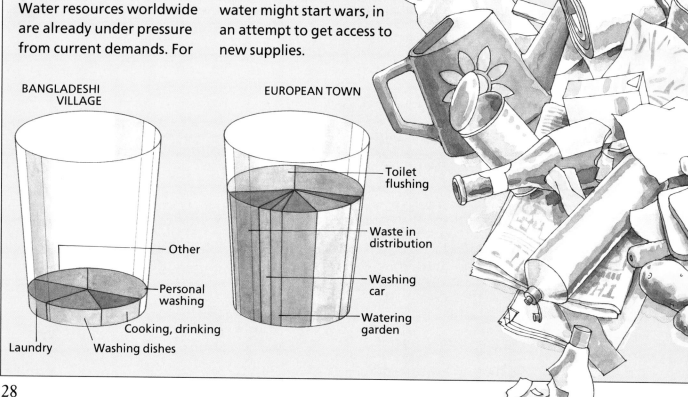

BANGLADESHI VILLAGE

EUROPEAN TOWN

- Toilet flushing
- Waste in distribution
- Washing car
- Watering garden

- Other
- Personal washing
- Cooking, drinking
- Laundry
- Washing dishes

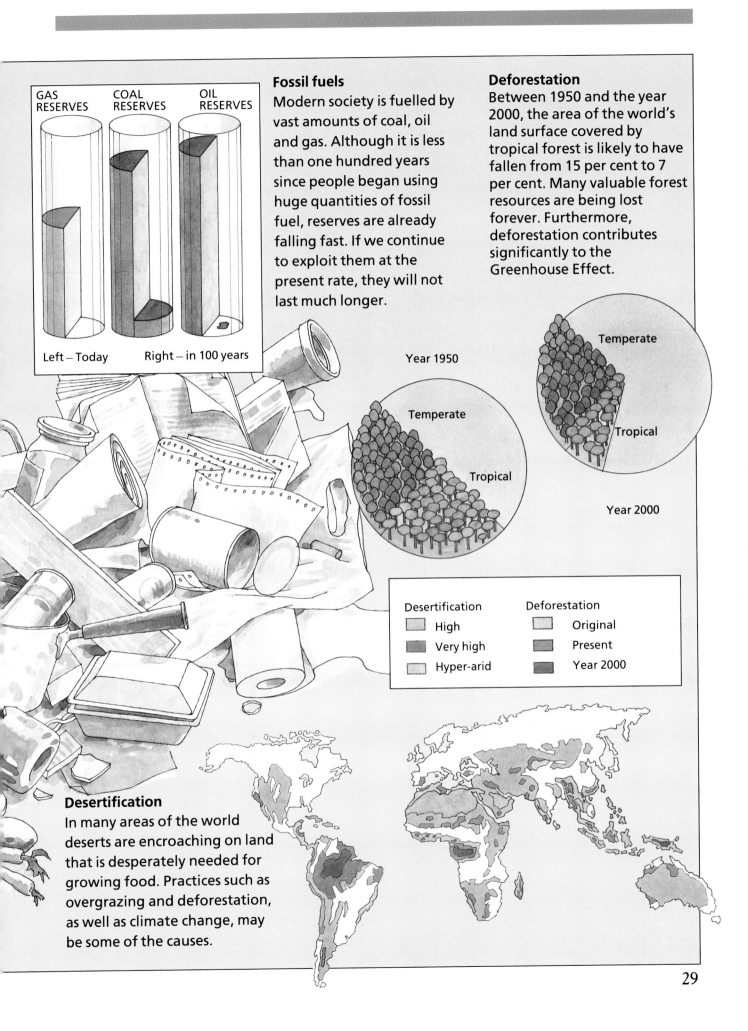

Fossil fuels

Modern society is fuelled by vast amounts of coal, oil and gas. Although it is less than one hundred years since people began using huge quantities of fossil fuel, reserves are already falling fast. If we continue to exploit them at the present rate, they will not last much longer.

GAS RESERVES COAL RESERVES OIL RESERVES

Left – Today   Right – in 100 years

Deforestation

Between 1950 and the year 2000, the area of the world's land surface covered by tropical forest is likely to have fallen from 15 per cent to 7 per cent. Many valuable forest resources are being lost forever. Furthermore, deforestation contributes significantly to the Greenhouse Effect.

Year 1950

Temperate

Tropical

Temperate

Tropical

Year 2000

Desertification
High
Very high
Hyper-arid

Deforestation
Original
Present
Year 2000

Desertification

In many areas of the world deserts are encroaching on land that is desperately needed for growing food. Practices such as overgrazing and deforestation, as well as climate change, may be some of the causes.

Chapter Four

WASTE NOT, WANT NOT

The human race is currently following a route which is simply not sustainable. In the last few hundred years, the world's population has grown explosively, colonising more and more natural wildernesses and resources. Population and economic growth, the main causes of escalating resource use, seem unstoppable. The problems involved are global, stretching across national borders regardless of political and social differences. Furthermore, the individual, caught up in day-to-day living, may hardly notice the damage being caused over the years. This is particularly true of the world's growing urban populations, who live surrounded by a manufactured environment and who have learned to take many of the products of resource exploitation for granted.

The world's changing landscape

To visualise the environmental damage being caused by resource exploitation, we should try to imagine Europe four hundred years ago. There were no tarmacked roads or railways, cities were much smaller and the countryside far wilder than it is now. Waterways were unpolluted and the air fresh and clear. Much of the land was carpeted in thick forests. Today, large amounts of the countryside are swallowed up by concrete and tarmac, and the last areas of wilderness are increasingly threatened by encroaching development.

On the other hand, much has improved in those four hundred years. Although the environment has been degraded by the escalation of resource use, our lifestyles are generally far healthier and more comfortable than in the 16th century, when most people lived shorter lives in squalid conditions that would today be quite unacceptable in the industrialised world.

In other areas of the world, a bird's eye view only 50 years ago would have included huge forests unbroken except by snaking grey rivers. Such sights today are increasingly difficult to find. Many of the

◁ While recycling paper at plants like this one (near left) does help save some trees, it will not help save forests where trees are felled to make way for the agricultural land needed to feed growing populations. Farming is the reason for the deforestation (pictured far left) in this valley in Nepal.

forests are now pitted and ragged – the result of accelerating deforestation. In the African interior a little more than one hundred years ago, the great plains were filled with herds of wild animals. Today, most of the remaining animals are restricted to a few game reserves.

Flying over India only one hundred years ago, we would have seen forests and plains, with some cultivation and a few cities and villages. Today, the vastly expanded population is putting land under increasing pressure. The extent of the changes that we have inflicted on landscapes around the world in a relatively short period is breathtaking: clearly the destruction cannot go on. We face the enormous tasks of renewing a balance with our environment and learning how to exploit the resources of the Earth in a sustainable way.

Recycling
In many developed countries, we waste many of the materials that pass through our hands. Many of us open a tin, empty its contents and toss it into the dustbin. It is strange to think how we have come to take such objects for granted. Our ancestors would have thought us mad to throw away this valuable metal; think of what they could have made from the materials used in the manufacture of an ordinary tin can.

Not only do we toss millions of tin cans into the bin every day, but we discard huge quantities of glass, plastic and paper. All represent some of the world's valuable resources and all are perfectly re-usable, yet we throw them out. Although recycling is becoming more common, there is still a lot more we could do.

All the metals we use can be melted down and re-used. The glass and much of the plastic we throw away can also be remoulded, and the paper can be pulped and remade. Much of the kitchen waste, like vegetable peelings, can be recycled by composting and used to nourish the garden instead of chemical fertilizers. Recycling not only helps to slow down the rate at which material resources are used up, but also helps to conserve valuable energy resources. Recycling aluminium only uses about five per cent of the energy required to smelt it from its ore.

Incentives
If we were to remove all the re-usable materials from our bins, very little would be left. Yet most of our domestic waste is buried or burned. Every re-usable object we throw away means that more resources are exploited to replace it. Unfortunately, there

31

is often little incentive to recycle materials and, in many cases, it is still cheaper to make metal, glass, plastic and paper from raw materials than it is to collect, sort and reprocess them. In other words, it is still cheaper to ransack natural resources than to use them sparingly and sensibly.

Growing concern about resources and the environment means that recycling is now beginning to be considered more seriously in Britain. Incentives to shift the balance between recycling and the production of new goods are gradually being introduced. In Sheffield, for example, a new scheme has been established to collect household refuse that has already been separated into paper, glass, metal and plastic and placed in special boxes on the pavement.

In the poorer nations where most people cannot afford new materials, recycling is very common. People use discarded objects like tyres, tin cans and light bulbs to make new and ingenious goods. Recycling is one way of conserving the world's resources. It means taking a long-term view and making the most of the limited raw materials available to us.

Conservation

Not everything can be recycled, however, particularly energy. Once energy has been used, it is lost. However, as with all resources, energy can be used more efficiently. At the moment, fossil fuels are still abundant, easily accessible and, consequently, still relatively cheap. Because of this, many homes and workplaces have not yet properly evaluated their energy use, and huge quantities of fossil fuels are being wasted unnecessarily. By making better use of energy through improved insulation of homes and offices, by using more efficient machinery, and by lighting and heating only when necessary, it is possible to cut fuel consumption drastically.

Some very large-scale schemes designed

to make better use of energy have already been developed. Many power stations, for example, waste huge amounts of energy in the form of hot water which they discharge into rivers and seas. A number of so-called Combined Heat and Power schemes now use this hot water to heat houses and offices. This type of conservation is likely to become more common as concern about the pollution caused by energy generation grows. Conservation does not only apply to energy. We can conserve any resource simply by using less of it. For example, if cars were made smaller and lighter this would conserve the amount of metal used in making them.

Substituting alternative materials

Another way of conserving materials is by finding substitutes for them. Developing substitute materials can ensure that the resource lasts much longer and that the material is used only where it is really needed. In the long run, oil may become an example of this. Currently we burn it for energy even though it is a vital resource for the chemical industry, and is also the raw material for the manufacture of thousands of products including medicines. Eventually we may find it desirable to use oil only as a raw material.

The need for international action

Global problems, like deforestation, the Greenhouse Effect, acid rain and the hole in the ozone layer, have become matters of grave concern worldwide. All are, in one way or another, linked with resource use. Deforestation is caused by cutting down trees to sell as timber or to make new agricultural land. The Greenhouse Effect and acid rain are predominantly the result of burning fossil fuel resources, and the hole in the ozone layer is the result of widespread emission of CFCs (chlorofluorocarbons) from fridges, air conditioning units and aerosol cans. Although recycling and conservation may help, they cannot completely solve these huge problems. We must find ways of using forest resources more sensibly. We should research how to generate energy without changing the composition of the atmosphere and we must build fridges that do not use CFCs.

The calls for action on global environmental problems are becoming stronger. It is difficult, however, to co-ordinate international agreements. This is particularly true in a world where nations compete in the international market-place. If a country decided to do something about the environment on its own, it would do it at considerable expense and its products would cost more.

Furthermore, many of the world's developing nations rightly argue that the industrial world grew wealthy through the uncontrolled exploitation of resources. Now that these countries have reaped such huge material benefits, it is easy for them to start calling for controls. Developing nations, which are at an earlier stage in their economic development, claim that they cannot be expected to slow the rate at which they use resources and often argue that they need to invest in their industries rather than improve their environmental record.

△ Scientists research the level of ozone in the atmosphere over Sweden.

◁ The Centre for Alternative Technology in Wales promotes new technologies and a lifestyle that makes better use of the limited resources available to us.

Our common future

In its 1987 report, "Our Common Future", the World Commission on Environment and Development detailed the most serious problems faced by people around the world, and suggested ways in which societies could develop sustainably. It has not yet triggered international action of the kind that is urgently needed.

△ Second-hand shops like this one are one way to recycle usable objects.

New ideas for a fairer world

It is going to take a lot of imagination to find a way around these problems. There is one increasingly popular suggestion to share resources more fairly. Economists have suggested that, as a way of reducing carbon dioxide emissions, every nation should be given strict emission quotas based on their populations and size.

Developing nations presently use less energy than the industrialised countries and as a result, many would not use their full quota. On the other hand, the quotas of the industrial nations would not be large enough to satisfy their energy demands. To solve this problem, quotas would be bought and sold on the open market. Industrial nations would have to pay to use so much energy. Energy conservation would then become desirable for every country. Nations which use less energy would benefit financially, while those who squandered energy would pay a heavy price.

Changing values

These types of measures may, however, prove insufficient. At the end of the day, we may need to change our attitudes to materialism. Many of the goods we surround ourselves with in the wealthy nations take a lot of energy and material to produce, although they are often not important to our basic comfort. We are using up valuable resources for no good reason and there is an urgent need to rethink our priorities. In this way we can safeguard the bulk of resources for the most useful and essential needs.

If we cannot find a way of reducing the damage caused by unrestrained use of resources, the result will be chaos. As materials and energy run short and we begin to suffer more from environmental degradation, it will be difficult to maintain the fabric of modern society. The challenge for human society is to develop a sustainable system before it is too late.

GLOSSARY

acid rain the result of sulphur dioxide and nitric oxide reacting with atmospheric water vapour and producing dilute solutions of nitric and sulphuric acid which fall as rain.

CFCs (chlorofluorocarbons) chemicals which are used for a variety of applications, including aerosols, fridges and the manufacture of some foam packaging.

developed countries countries with economies based around their industrial capacity and in which factories provide more jobs than agriculture. Compared to developing countries, income per person is high and provision of health care, education and social services is good, but some people still live in poverty.

developing countries countries with little industry and mainly rural economies. Average incomes are generally far lower than those in the industrialised nations and health and education provision is often poor. Conditions obviously vary greatly between different countries.

ecosystem self-regulating natural community of plants and animals interacting with themselves and with their environment.

fertilizer a substance containing chemical elements necessary for healthy plant growth and used to compensate for poor soil or soil depleted by repeated cropping.

fossil fuel fuel composed of the fossilised remnants of plants and micro-organisms. Coal, gas and oil are all fossil fuels.

Greenhouse Effect the process by which certain gases (greenhouse gases) in the Earth's atmosphere trap heat from the Sun, keeping the planet's surface warm enough for life. Greenhouse gases added to the atmosphere by human activities threaten to enhance the atmosphere's ability to trap heat and could lead to global warming.

hectare a measure of land area. There are 100 hectares in one square kilometre.

Industrial Revolution characterised by the development of manufacturing industries and a rapid escalation of resource use. Began in Britain in the 18th century and quickly spread across Europe and North America, accelerating throughout the 19th century.

non-renewable resources resources that can only be extracted once (for example, metals and fossil fuels).

ore minerals from which metals (and some non-metals) are profitably extracted.

ozone layer a layer which exists in the atmosphere at a height of between 15 and 30 km which contains a high concentration of ozone. This layer filters out harmful ultraviolet radiation from the Sun.

organic produce produce grown on land which has had no artificial fertilizers or pesticides applied to it for at least two years and where crop rotation and natural inputs are used.

pesticide substance used in the control of pests. There are three main types of pesticides; herbicides, fungicides and insecticides which are designed to kill weeds, fungi and insects. Many pesticides are harmful to people, particularly when they enter the food chain.

photosynthesis process by which plants use the energy of the Sun for growth.

renewable resources resources that regenerate themselves (for example, wind, wood, fish).

sustainable society a society which uses resources in such a way that it can continue to support the current lifestyle of its population indefinitely.

INDEX

Photographic Credits:
Cover and pages 6 left, 15, 17 right, 18 left, 23 left and right: Robert Harding Library; intro page and pages 4, 6 right, 7, 8, 13 right, 14 both, 18 right, 21 bottom, 25, 26 and 27 top: J. Allan Cash Library; pages 9, 19, 21 top and 30: Hutchinson Library; page 13 left: The Mansell Collection; page 16-17: Associated Press/Topham; page 20: Popperfoto; page 27 bottom: Eye Ubiquitous; page 28-29: Frank Spooner Agency.